HORSES

THOROUGHBRED HORSES

by Alissa Thielges

AMICUS

back legs

track

Look for these words and pictures as you read.

braid

polo

What is that fast horse?
It is a Thoroughbred!

These horses work hard.
They are good at many things.

See the back legs?
They are strong.
The horse runs hard.

back legs

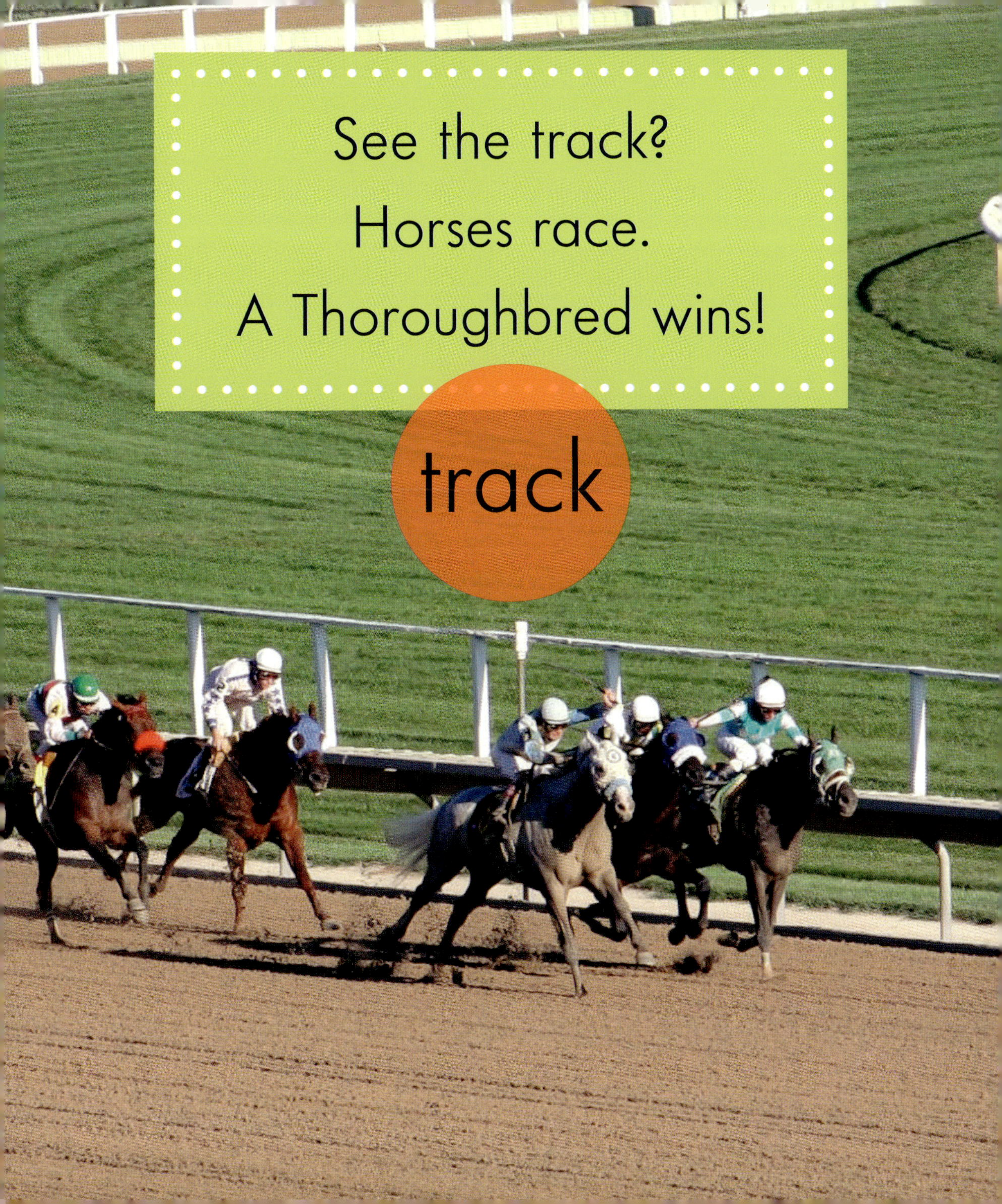
See the track?
Horses race.
A Thoroughbred wins!
track

See the button braid?
The mane looks neat.
It is for a show.

braid

See the rider?
He is on a Thoroughbred.
He plays polo.
He hits the ball. Goal!

polo

A Thoroughbred jumps.
Great job!

Did you find?

back legs

track

braid

polo

Spot is published by Amicus
P.O. Box 227, Mankato, MN 56002
www.amicuspublishing.us

Library of Congress Cataloging-in-Publication Data
Names: Thielges, Alissa, 1995- author.
Title: Thoroughbred horses / by Alissa Thielges.
Description: Mankato, Minnesota : Amicus, [2023] | Series: Spot horses | Includes bibliographical references and index. | Audience: Ages 4-7 | Audience: Grades K-1 | Summary: "Meet the Thoroughbred horse breed in this leveled reader that reinforces key vocabulary with a search-and-find feature. Carefully controlled text and excellent photos introduce these fast horses to early readers. "—Provided by publisher.
Identifiers: LCCN 2021055473 (print) | LCCN 2021055474 (ebook) | ISBN 9781645492498 (hardcover) | ISBN 9781681527734 (paperback) | ISBN 9781645493372 (ebook)
Subjects: LCSH: Thoroughbred horse--Juvenile literature.
Classification: LCC SF293.T5 T38 2023 (print) | LCC SF293.T5 (ebook) | DDC 636.1/32--dc23/eng/20211213
LC record available at https://lccn.loc.gov/2021055473
LC ebook record available at https://lccn.loc.gov/2021055474

Rebecca Glaser, editor
Deb Miner, series designer
Catherine Berthiaume and Grant Gould, book design and photo research

Photos by Alamy/Juniors Bildarchiv GmbH, cover, 16, GFC Collection 12-13; Pxhere 8-9; Shutterstock/Diane Bliessen 1, Jesus Cervantes 3, 6-7, Fotokostic 4-5, taylon 10-11, Zuzule 14-15